Cliques
Deal with it
using what you have inside

Kat Mototsune • Illustrated by Ben Shannon

James Lorimer & Company Ltd., Publishers
Toronto

It's just another day
at school and all around you
are the usual players.

Each table in the lunchroom has a different bunch of kids sitting at it—the jocks, the music and arts kids, the emos, the science nerds. Every time people get together it can be called a group, but there seem to be definite rules about who belongs where and who does not.

When people form groups with rules and expectations for members, the groups can be called cliques.

Cliques have the power to include and exclude.

That in-crowd of girls over there make up a clique. You know, they're not necessarily the prettiest, or the smartest, or the most athletic. Not all of them have important parents or families with money. But, somehow, every boy wants them to notice him, and every girl wants to belong to their clique. They're the ones who decide what it's cool to do, what to wear, and what to be interested in.

So how does a clique decide who belongs and who doesn't?

Why can clique members be nice to some kids while victimizing or completely ignoring others? Where exactly does that power come from?

If you want to know the ins and outs of cliques, this book can help.

Contents

What is a Clique?

Everyone has groups of people to do things or spend time with. You might have groups of friends based on:

- your hobbies or interests
- your ethnic or racial background
- where you live
- the sports or games you play
- the music you listen to
- the blogs you read or write

But cliques want to control everything about the life of their members:

- who belongs and who doesn't
- what to wear
- who you can be friendly with
- who to be mean to or ignore
- what opinions you can express
- what secrets you have to keep
- who you can network with online

When being part of the group is more important than what brought the individuals together, it's a clique. Cliques don't put up with any one member being different or not following the rules they have established. Cliques are often more about who to keep out than who to let in.

Cliques 101

Omar usually eats lunch with his best friend, Sam.

But once he makes the basketball team...

Cliques decide who to...

Thanks for the new computer, Mom.

Look, all the girls in my class are online!

This is Genna, the new girl. She just moved in down the street from me.

The class will vote on one student to represent us at the mock parliament.

Cliques 101

QUIZ

Group or Clique — what's the difference?
People naturally like to hang out together—it's part of what makes us people. We form groups based on many things, from close friendships to belonging to the same club or team. So how do you know if a group is really a clique? A lot of the time, it has to do with how a clique treats people, including its members. Read the following scenarios and decide if each is an example of a **Group** or a **Clique**. Check your answers on the opposite page.

1

The hip-hop dance class meets every other day after school, but the members don't eat lunch together.

2

Kimi and her school friends are constantly texting each other, but she isn't allowed to give her number to the girls on her soccer team, because her friends don't think her teammates are cool enough.

3

Corey and his friends use code names for each person in their class, so that they can text each other about their classmates without others knowing.

4

When Chelsea makes the rep hockey team, the guys invite her to join in their weekend shinny games.

5

When Patrick gets teased by the class bully, Ben and his group of art friends let Patrick eat lunch with them.

6

Raoul has to sneak into the school and tag lockers if he wants to hang with the b-boys.

7

When Ming fails his Social Studies test, he has to stay out of the Academics Club until he improves his marks.

Academics Club 4 P.M. today! B there or B ec2

8

Brit aced her math test, and now the girls she hangs out with won't speak to her unless she lets them copy her homework.

9

The girls all play on a website where they collect virtual accessories to dress up their avatars. Darla tells her friends to transfer the things they have collected to her account, or she will block them from the chats they have.

10

Noor's friends don't like her new boyfriend, but they make sure she knows they won't exclude her for that.

Answers

1. Group   6. Clique
2. Clique   7. Group
3. Clique   8. Clique
4. Group   9. Clique
5. Group   10. Group

Cliques 101

Dear Clique Counsellor

Q: I've just started middle school and I'm ready to be part of the popular clique. I've worked out, spent loads of money on the right clothes and gadgets, dropped all my friends who weren't cool enough, and joined all the right teams and clubs. But I still can't break into the group of kids who are better-dressed, richer, and cooler than everyone else. What gives?

— *Wannabe*

A: It sounds like you decide on a course of action and see it through. That's something to be proud of, especially if you are happy about all the changes you've made to yourself. But you have to ask yourself who decided what is "right" about you now, and what was "wrong" about you to begin with. How much are you willing to change yourself to fit in with a clique? And even if they decide that you have what it takes to belong, what about the kids who used to be your friends? You just might find that you were happier belonging with them than belonging to a clique whose members don't care who you really are.

Q: After the spring break, the girls I hang out with decided on a bunch of rules—who we can talk to, what we should wear, what activities are cool enough, who we can give our cell numbers to, what subjects in school we can do well in, even how to talk. I like belonging to a clique, but does it really mean that we all have to be exactly the same?
— CC

A: It sounds like these girls really like belonging to a clique and value the fact that you are one of them, too. But I notice that you don't call these girls your friends. If they were really your friends, they would encourage and value the things that make you you. Sometimes it is easier to get along if you don't stand out from the people around you, and it's clear that the other girls in your clique lack the self-confidence to stand out in any way. You can talk to them and ask if the list of rules can be shortened, or if there is any leeway at all. But if you think that the way you do things is just right for you, you have to stand up for yourself, even if it means being excluded. It's your call. Good luck!

Q: My problem is with the boys' basketball team. The coach suggested I try out for the team, but at tryouts the rest of the team worked together to keep the ball away from me and fouled me when the coach wasn't looking. I was as surprised as anyone when the coach told me I made the team. But now the guys trip me in the hallways, shout put-downs across the schoolyard, and break into my locker and mess with my stuff. What should I do?
— Being B-Ball Bullied

A: I know it doesn't mean much, but good for you for trying out in the first place. Obviously, the guys on the basketball team still don't feel you belong in their clique, even though the coach kept you on the team. They feel their power as a team is threatened by the coach's decision. So they are trying to make sure that everyone knows they rule. They are trying to keep the team strong, but picking on you also means that they can't add your strength to the team. Another good call on your part is identifying what is happening to you as bullying. In many cases, you can stop a clique from victimizing you by staying out of their way and lying low. But the physical violence and vandalism mean you have to address this as a bullying problem: confide in an adult you can trust (the coach, if possible), talk to other kids to see if anyone else is being bullied, avoid and ignore the guys on the basketball team when you can, and be assertive (not aggressive) when you have to deal with them face-to-face.

Q: Some girls at my school have set up a website that says nasty things about a lot of the kids and teachers. Only the girls involved are supposed to know about it, but I stumbled across it one day while I was surfing for school activities. Do you think the things on the website are true?
— Wondering

A: It's a good thing that this website bothers you. It's cyberbullying, and it's wrong. Whether or not the things are true, the girls think the website gives them power to share "secrets" about other people. They are using it to hurt others. So what do you do with the power that comes from knowing their secret? That's up to you, and depends on what kind of person you decide to be. Do you want to be the kind of person that lets people be mean and aggressive to others, or the kind of person that stands up to bullying and tries to stop it? Cyberbullying is also abuse of the Internet—you might want to let an adult know so that a closer eye may be kept on the computer privileges of the girls.

Myths

Belonging is everything.

Belonging to a clique can make you feel like you're not alone, but not all cliques are created equal. The best way to belong is by still being you.

These are the best friends you'll ever have.

This might be true, but only if none of you ever grow up, change, or become the best adults you can make yourselves. As you change, so will your friendships.

There is strength in numbers.

People do feel more powerful as part of a group. But what counts is how that power is used. Real strength is the ability to help people, not hurt and victimize them.

Only girls can make up a clique.

While a lot of cliques are made up of girls, there are boy cliques, too. And sometimes cliques can contain both boys and girls.

DID YOU KNOW?

- In a recent U.S. survey of teenage girls' views of cliques, 96.3 percent of the respondents claimed that cliques existed in their schools.

Only **popular** kids are in **cliques.**

Like all groups of people, cliques form anytime people have things in common. There are all sorts of cliques, and clique members are always popular—at least with other members of their clique!

People are **happier** in cliques.

Every clique has rules to make sure that the members are all doing the same thing, but those rules can make individual members unhappy if it means they are not free to be themselves or to express how they feel or think.

Some people are **born leaders.**

Most cliques have a leader, but the only power they have is what's given to them by their followers.

- Cliques can consist of up to 12 kids, with an average of 4–5.

- Cliques aren't just for girls. Guys form cliques too—usually around a sport, computer game, or type of clothing or music. They can be just as mean as girls to the outcasts of the social group.

The Outsider

Where do I belong?

You wonder why cliques don't even seem to see you, never mind include you. Or, worse yet, maybe they gang up on you to make your life miserable.

Why does the world seem to be run by cliques? What does a kid have to do to be accepted around here, anyway?

DEAR DR. SHRINK-WRAPPED...

Q: I don't know what to do. I really wanted to hang with the glee club and the musical kids in our grade, but they always ignored me. Then one day, Ashlee, the best singer and dancer in the clique, sent me an e-mail saying that she was auditioning new members and I was being considered. I was so happy! But they never asked me to sing. Instead, Ashlee kept e-mailing me all week, asking me what I thought about other girls in our grade. She said some nasty things about some of them, even my friends, and I agreed with her. I even made up some stuff about girls I didn't know too well—anything to get a chance to sing! Well, the day the glee club was going to announce who was in, I got to school and found that the girls in my grade had stuffed my locker with hate notes and garbage. It turns out Ashlee had printed out our e-mails, deleting her parts, and given copies of my insults to all the girls. Now everyone hates me, and the glee club members laugh every time they see me. My life at this school is over.

— *Wannabe Wanna-change-schools*

A: Wanna, you worked so hard to follow your dream and to show your talent. I agree that the way Ashlee treated you was completely unfair. Ashlee played a really rotten trick on you, and maybe you were so blinded by the chance to be accepted by her that you did some pretty awful things, too. Dr. Shrink-Wrapped can see why you'd want to start all over again at a new school, but that might not be possible, or even the best thing—you might find yourself being a Wannabe of another clique just like the glee club.

Dr. Shrink-Wrapped suggests that you take a step back in time, before all this happened, and think about what was good then. You had some real friends, right? If you give up trying to be accepted by people who only want to hurt you for fun, you can try to get back what you had before. First, approach your old friends and tell them the whole story. This will be tough, and you have to think more about their feelings than your own. You will have to admit you made a big mistake and try to repair the damage you have done to your friendships. But if they were your friends, they know how much you wanted to fit in with the glee club. They might still be

mad about the things you revealed in your e-mails to Ashlee, but if you can prove to them that you are genuinely sorry and that you value their friendship, they might take you back. And as for the rest of the girls in your grade, give it some time. Soon, there will be a whole new scandal, and you can go back to being ignored by everyone but your real friends.

Q: The guys on the swim team rule our school. Because I was really overweight, my doctor, my parents, and my friends got me started on swimming to improve my health. The trouble is, I couldn't avoid the swim team at the pool. They called me "Whale" and hid my clothes. I shot off a few taunts about their brains being waterlogged and left it at that. My friends stuck by me, and I stuck with it. I'm still big, but my health is a lot better. Problem is, the treatment from the swim team is getting worse, and it's not just at the pool anymore. The swim guys push and shove me in the change room when my friends aren't there. They've started leaving pictures of whaling boats and bloody whales on my desk. I even found a toy harpoon in my locker! Why are they being such jerks, and what can I do to get them to leave me alone?

— *Moby Dick*

A: Dr. Shrink-Wrapped wants to start by congratulating you on taking your health into your own hands—or swim fins! Moby, you sound like a very cool kid to me—with a sense of humour and people who care about you. You also aren't that impressed with the swim team, and that might be why they are bullying you. People in cliques often think that making others look bad will make them look better and feel stronger, so they often put down other people. Dr. Shrink-Wrapped's advice is to not let those fish sticks know that you are upset or scared. Stick with people who support you and care about you. Try to have friends meet you in the change room after your swim, since the pushing and shoving might stop if there are witnesses. If things get worse or more violent, tell an adult you can trust about the bullying that is going on.

QUIZ

How do you deal with being on the outside looking in?

When it comes to cliques you are definitely not a part of, do you Wannabe included? Do you find that you're a Victim? Or are you happy By Yourself? Choose the answer that best suits you to find out how you let cliques affect your life.

1 FACE TIME

You know that the members of a certain clique at school all have presences on the same social network. How do you react?

A) So what? You're fine with the friends you have online and off.
B) You try to friend the leaders of the clique.
C) You try to friend the members of the clique, but you find that you are on their list of people to block.

2 INTEREST IN YOUR FUTURE

Your dad is worried that you aren't socializing with the right kids at school and wants you to hang out with the athletic kids—but they're cliquey. What do you do?

A) Do whatever you can to make yourself just like they are.
B) Continue on with your old friends. Who needs to be a jock?
C) Go out of your way to get the attention of the clique. Even if they are calling you names and pulling pranks on you, at least they are noticing you.

3 EATING DISS-ORDER

The fashionista girls in your grade have decided that all girls have to be the perfect weight, or they will put your name on a list on their blog. What do you do?

A) Run away when they suggest that throwing up might be a good way for you to handle your weight problem.
B) Ignore them—a person's weight is nobody else's business.
C) Tell the fashionistas that they are right and that you are going to lose as much weight as it takes to make yourself prettier and more popular.

4 Tangled Web

A clique in your grade has set up a website about a girl in your class and how much everyone hates her. Included are links to a website full of nasty comments about the kids who don't post vicious things on the original website.

A) You post nasty comments about the girl right away.
B) You cry when you follow the links and find bad things posted about you.
C) You wonder what the girl did to make people be so mean to her, so you can make sure not to do the same thing.

5 POPULARITY CON-TEST

Your teacher gives a group assignment where you have to apply to join a group. Everyone groups up according to their usual cliques—the jocks, the science nerds, the trendies. The teacher says that since social skills are a learning goal, anyone who does the assignment alone will have marks deducted. The problem is that you don't belong to any of the cliques in the class. What do you do?

A) You approach every clique and beg to be included.
B) You lie on your application.
C) You don't bother applying for a group and work alone. Who needs the extra marks?

TEXT TEASE

You start getting texts that look like they are from the cutest guy in your class. But your best friend says she thinks they are really being sent by a clique of girls that includes his ex-girlfriend. Your reaction?

A) You ignore the texts and change your number.
B) You figure your friend must be jealous, so you get up your nerve to approach the cute guy and thank him for noticing you.
C) You ignore your friend's warnings and show the texts to the clique—if you are good enough for him, you should be able to hang with them.

 ## Conference Call Complications

The leader of the brainy girls phones and leaves a message saying that she wants your opinion on a friend of yours, because you are both being considered to join the class Mensa club. A girl in your class warns you that it might be a trick.

A) You tell the smart girl in person that you would be a much better choice than your friend, and make up reasons.
B) You don't return the message and cool things off with your friend to avoid the attention of the clique.
C) You call the smart girl back, but your friend is listening as part of a conference call to the things you say about her. Now your friend hates you and the clique is spreading the news about what a bad friend you are.

Tough Talk

Your friend has a speech impediment that makes him hard to understand sometimes. You are sitting with him in the lunchroom, when the hip-hop clique starts making fun of the way he talks and calling him a "retard." They ask you if you want to come sit with them instead.

A) You leave the lunchroom and leave your friend sitting alone. Who needs that kind of attention?
B) You stick with your friend, even when they start putting you down, too.
C) You join the b-kids and laugh about your friend's impediment.

 ## Race RELATIONS

The clique of black kids is having a put-down war with the academic Asian kids you usually hang with. You are of mixed race, and both cliques want you to join them for a shout-down in the schoolyard. What do you do?

A) No contest—you side with the black kids and avoid your Asian friends.
B) You hide in the library for as long as it takes to blow over.
C) You stick with your friends and put up with the black kids singling you out for extra abuse.

Poll-litical Perils

The skateboarders are going to poll everyone in your grade about which girls are "sluts" and which are "bitches." They are going to post the results on a blog.

A) You stay home sick the day the poll is being taken.
B) You make up horrible things to tell them about all the girls except your friends.
C) You refuse to say bad things about your friends, so they put your name in as both a slut and a bitch.

Answers

1. A) By Yourself
    B) Wannabe
    C) Victim
2. A) Wannabe
    B) By Yourself
    C) Victim
3. A) Victim
    B) By Yourself
    C) Wannabe
4. A) Wannabe
    B) Victim
    C) By Yourself
5. A) Victim
    B) Wannabe
    C) By Yourself
6. A) By Yourself
    B) Victim
    C) Wannabe
7. A) Wannabe
    B) By Yourself
    C) Victim
8. A) By Yourself
    B) Victim
    C) Wannabe
9. A) Wannabe
    B) By Yourself
    C) Victim
10. A) By Yourself
    B) Wannabe
    C) Victim

What's It Worth?

You might think you would do anything to be part of a clique. But what is belonging worth? Is it worth sacrificing your real friendships? Going against what you feel is right? Putting someone else in danger or making someone else a victim? Belonging to a clique is only the right thing if you can . . .

Be Yourself

All cliques have rules, and following those rules might mean that you aren't able to make the decisions you want to make. If being accepted into a clique stops you from being the person you really are—or want to be—then you are letting other people decide who you are. And there is nothing cool about that.

Be a Real Friend

You probably know what it is to have a real friend, and to be a real friend. Often, a clique will not want you to be close to anyone but other members of the clique. They might try to get you to say or do mean things to a friend who is not included. But do you want to be friends with people who ask you to abandon your real friends?

Be Fair

If a clique has treated you badly, you know that they don't need a reason to target you. Maybe they think making you look bad makes them look better. But you know better than to believe that. If you want to be part of a clique, make sure you stick to treating other people fairly.

Have Your Own Power

Being part of a clique is all about having power— power over the other members of the clique, and power over people outside of the clique. After all, they decide who to shut out and who to target. But a clique only has as much power as you let it have. Whether inside or outside a clique, you always have the power to make your own decisions and treat people the way you feel is right.

DID YOU KNOW?

• One out of six girls deliberately hides her intelligence and interest in doing well at school out of the desire to be accepted by other kids.

do's and don'ts

✓ Do stick with people who have the same interests and values as you.

✓ Do believe in yourself and your own decisions.

✓ Do avoid groups of kids who instigate conflict with you.

✓ Do realize that having real friends is better than being included by people who don't know you.

✓ Do spend time with people who are positive and self-confident.

✓ Do treat everyone with respect.

✓ Do respect yourself.

✓ Do explore your own interests.

✓ Do remember that other people's values may be different from yours, and may influence the way they act.

✗ Don't believe everything you are told about other people.

✗ Don't let lies told about yourself make you feel bad or wrong.

✗ Don't confuse popularity with friendship.

✗ Don't let other people tell you who you want to be.

✗ Don't admire people just because they're popular.

✗ Don't choose who to follow out of fear.

✗ Don't change who you really are to fit in with a clique.

✗ Don't spend all your money on stuff just to fit in.

✗ Don't break the rules—or the law— to get approval.

✗ Don't be afraid to talk to an adult if the way others treat you becomes unbearable.

• When kids were asked which group they would like to belong to, five times as many students selected the "populars" or "jocks" as chose the "brains."

• While boys are more aggressive than girls physically, studies show that boys are just as likely as girls to use tactics like gossiping, spreading rumours, and isolating others.

Birds of a **feather** flock together.

Hey, it's natural for kids to want to hang with others like them. Whether you are with the jocks or the preps, the glee club or the geeks, the freaks or the fashionistas, it's pretty much your group against the rest of the world. And if you are smart or athletic or fashionable enough to be friends with the other cool kids, what's wrong with that?

My group of friends is a clique? **Really?**

It's not like being part of a clique means you spend all your time being nasty to other people or working at staying in good with the rest of the clique.

But think about it. Do you ever find yourself going along with your friends when you would rather be doing or saying what you really feel like? Do you make all your decisions based on the rules of the group? Maybe you even find that everyone in your clique looks to you to take the lead, and it's just easier to repeat the behaviour that keeps some kids in and some kids out?

Being inside a clique can be even worse than being alone, if you feel you can't be yourself.

do's and don'ts

✓ Do realize that everyone is different.

✓ Do try to make friends outside your own group.

✓ Do make up your own mind about what is important.

✓ Do disagree with your friends if they are treating others badly.

✓ Do explore your own interests.

✓ Do treat everyone with respect.

✓ Do treat other kids as individuals, not as members of groups.

✓ Do remember that other people's values may be different from yours, and may influence the way they act.

✓ Do realize that, as a group, you and your friends might have the power to influence other people.

✓ Do use that influence to help people feel good about themselves.

✓ Do try to include new friends with your usual group.

✗ Don't expect everyone to want to be just like you.

✗ Don't use the fact that people look up to you to make them feel bad.

✗ Don't think that you look better if you make someone else look bad.

✗ Don't tell other people's secrets to get power over them.

✗ Don't use your popularity to spread rumours about other people.

✗ Don't change who you really are to fit in with a group.

✗ Don't spend all your money on stuff just to fit in.

✗ Don't break the rules—or the law—to get approval from your friends.

✗ Don't be ashamed to disagree with the opinions of your friends.

✗ Don't make people do or say things just because you can.

✗ Don't let other people decide what should be important to you.

✗ Don't let your friends decide who you can associate with.

QUIZ

Are you Mean Girls or Guys?

Whether you are the one who makes decisions in your clique or you are just working hard at belonging, what makes you need to be an insider? Take this quiz to see what you can find out. Of the following statements, how many are **true**, and how many are **false**?

1. I can tell if people are like me just by looking at them.

2. There are a lot of geeks and losers at my school.

3. I don't like being around people who are not like me.

4. My friends look to me to make decisions for all of us.

5. There are rules to follow in my group of friends.

6. I tease people if they look or act differently from me and my friends.

7. There are people who simply don't belong with us.

8. If my friends know what I'm really like, they wouldn't spend time with me.

9. The worse other people look, the better I will look.

10. I don't like to disagree with the people around me.

11. I don't like standing out from my friends.

12. A group of people has more power than a single individual.

I've been mean to people because my friends expect it of me. **13**

Sometimes I hide what I really think and feel from my friends. **14**

Being popular is more important than being liked. **15**

Having people want to be like you is more important than being liked. **16**

My friends are all like me. **17**

I get people to tell me their secrets and then I use what I know against them. **16**

It is important for me to act a certain way in front of my friends. **19**

I go to school mostly to connect with my friends. **20**

Everyone falls into one of just a few categories. **21**

I need to dress like my friends. **22**

It's better for people to fear me than to like me. **23**

I've done things to people outside my group of friends that I'm ashamed of. **24**

I know what I have to do to keep my friends. **25**

Did you score a lot of trues? Maybe it's time to think about why fitting in with your clique is more important than being who you really are.

How to Make Your Clique Click

Nobody is telling you that you shouldn't have a group of friends or that you can't belong to a clique. But how do the people around you treat others that they feel don't belong? How do they treat you when you disagree with them? How do you feel when you are in the group—good about yourself, or like you have to be someone else to fit in? In any case, there are ways that you can stay part of the clique and make sure that your friends are popular for all the right reasons.

Break Out.

You might feel like the time you spend with the clique is great, but there are things that you want to do and talk about with other people— people who see you as something beyond just a member of a clique. Don't be afraid to go outside the clique sometimes. Spending time with people who have different ideas and interests makes you a cooler person, and that makes the clique cooler.

Loosen up.

It's great to surround yourself with people who support you, but it's not a good thing if you lack the self-confidence to be anything but a copy of every other member of the group. See if you can loosen up the rules of the clique, or introduce new ways of doing things. You might end up with a happier group of people to spend time with.

Look around.

It's the nature of a clique that some people are "in" and the rest have to be "out"—it's right there in the definition. But have a look at how you treat people who are "out" when your clique is all together. Is it different from how you would act toward them if you were alone? If you tease and bully outsiders, then ask yourself why your clique uses its power to hurt others instead of influencing them to be better—more like you!

DID YOU KNOW?

- North American teens spend more time with friends each day than in any other activity.

- Time spent with friends increases from 25% in Grade 5 to 40% in Grade

Be a leader.

If you find that everyone in your clique looks to you for guidance, you can choose how to use those great leadership skills. When you are making rules for the clique—from who to include to how much individuality each member can show—it's up to you to decide if the clique is going to be admired or feared. Do you have the self-confidence to turn you and your friends into a super-group??

If each member of your clique is the best person possible, that makes your clique the best it can be. And who wouldn't want to belong to a group like that?

When Gangs are Involved

What's the difference between a clique and a gang? They have many things in common. Members of both cliques and gangs:
- have a sense of belonging
- often wear the same type of clothes, colours, hairstyles, or things like tattoos
- have similar interests
- often share an ethnicity, economic background, or neighbourhood
- feel close, like they are a family
- keep secrets and protect each other
- can be aggressive and abusive to outsiders and members of other groups

Most of all, cliques and gangs are alike because there is a clear line dividing those who belong from those who don't.

The big difference is this: gangs operate on the wrong side of the law. Gang activity often includes crime and violence. Like cliques, gangs exclude, but once you are in a gang, it is inclusion that has the highest stakes. The rules are much more rigid, and breaking them brings more serious—and often dangerous—consequences. And it might be almost impossible to leave without risking your safety or even your life.

It can be hard to say no if a gang is pressuring you to join. But think about the ways that being part of a gang could change your life—for the worse:
- you will probably be expected to break the law, and may even go to jail
- you will have to hurt anyone the gang has issues with
- you will have to obey the gang, even if it causes problems with your home life and family
- the gang will have to be more important than school, a job, or a future career
- you could get hurt or killed

Gangs, like cliques, are successful because people are willing to do things in a group that they might be too afraid or too sensible to do on their own. A gang might seem to support you, but where the law is concerned, you will someday have to take responsibility for your own actions.

- Not everyone is part of a clique. Some kids have close friends in different cliques, but do not belong to a particular clique themselves. Some kids have few friends, inside or outside of cliques.

- Being able to form friendships is not necessarily connected to being part of a clique; some kids who are highly accepted by cliques have no close friendships, while over half of the kids who are not highly accepted by cliques have close friends.

You're happy to be flying under the radar of all the cliques around you.

Sure, you have friends. But you are quite happy to avoid the drama of cliques.

You've probably been around when a clique has ganged up to exclude or tease someone. Maybe someone you know is desperate to be accepted by a clique, and has said or done things they wouldn't normally say or do to make that happen. Did you say or do anything? Well, why not?

Are you an Ostrich?

Especially at school, cliques tend to rule most people's lives. So how are you avoiding dealing with cliques? If you are hiding your head in the sand to escape the notice of cliques, you might

- not stand up for what you really believe
- throw someone else "under the bus" to make a clique choose another victim
- stand by while someone is being victimized by a clique

What you are doing is letting clique behaviour affect who you are as much as if you were the one being teased and bullied. You are not a loser, so don't let the clique make you into one.

Or a Lone Wolf?

You don't need the validation of people you don't really like, and you have enough self-confidence to keep you from becoming a target of the cliques. But think about what you might be missing by avoiding groups that might help you do some good in your own world. Cliques and groups gather for a wide range of reasons, with criminal gangs on one end and groups of real friends on the other. If you look into running with a pack, you might find or form a group of people who

- accept who you really are
- support your right to make decisions, even if they might disagree with them
- not use your friendship for their own selfish means

With friends like that, who needs to be alone?

do's and don'ts

✓ Do stand up for what you really believe in.

✓ Do value the differences between people.

✓ Do try to deal with individuals, not groups.

✓ Do support those around you who are being victimized by cliques.

✓ Do speak up if you disagree with how cliques are treating people.

✓ Do respect everyone's right to decide who they want to associate with.

✓ Do accept and respect your friends' right to make their own decisions.

✗ Don't hide from cliques at all costs.

✗ Don't help a clique victimize someone to avoid being teased or bullied yourself.

✗ Don't make assumptions about individuals based on the groups they belong to.

✗ Don't believe or spread gossip.

✗ Don't go along with people if you disagree with their behaviour.

✗ Don't get involved when cliques come into conflict.

✗ Don't let a conflict escalate to hurtfulness or violence.

QUIZ

Do you really get it?

It's hard to know what to do when cliques get out of hand. But you do have choices! What would you do in the following situations? This quiz has no right or wrong answers, because each situation—and every person—is different. Your answers might be different from the ones suggested here, but they may be right, under the circumstances.

1 SKIPPING SISTER

Your younger sister wants to hang with the popular girls in her grade. They tell her that she can join their clique if she skips school part of every day for a week, which would include missing one test.

2 SHE AIN'T HEAVY

Your friend is overweight. In the change room after gym class, you see a girl take a picture of your friend naked. That girl sends the picture to her clique, and you hear that they are planning to send it to every boy in your grade.

- Tell your friend, and tell her you will go with her if she wants to report it to an adult.
- If you feel safe, speak up. Call the girls out for picking on your friend.
- Tell the gym teacher right away. See if the teacher can take the camera to make sure the picture is deleted.

- Talk to your sister and try to find out why it is so important for her to belong to the clique. Offer to spend more time with her, and be supportive of her making good decisions about her friends.
- Remind her that she shouldn't risk getting in trouble with the school. Without threatening to tell on her, remind her that if your parents find out, she will be in big trouble with them, too.
- Encourage her to ask the clique if there's another way to prove that she is worthy to be included.
- Tell your parents that your sister is being pressured by the clique, and see if they will gently talk to her about the kinds of friends she should be seeking out.

3 RUNAWAY BOYFRIEND

Your boyfriend has made it onto the track and field team. He says that the rest of the team won't let him go out with girls who are not athletic, and they will find him a hotter girlfriend. He cares about you and doesn't know what to do.

- Let your boyfriend go. If belonging with the team is more important to him than you are, that's his decision.
- Ask your boyfriend if he wants to cut down on the time you spend together, and just see each other when the other members of the team won't know.
- Tell him that he has to choose between you and the team.
- Tell him that if he wants to dump you for a prettier girl, he shouldn't blame the team.

4 HIP-HOP BRO

While checking out an amateur video website, you come across an embarrassing video of your little brother pretending to be a rapper. You know that a group of kids in his class have been targeting and teasing a lot of people this way.

- Tell your brother. Help him contact the site to have the video removed.
- Try to help your brother deal with the teasing he'll be getting. Remind him that he has real friends, and that the teasing will eventually stop when they find someone else to tease.
- Find out who took the video and uploaded it to the website. Have a talk with the kids involved about how Internet abuse can get them into trouble.

5 PHONE PHONY

Your science fair partner is all excited because the cutest guy in your grade left her a voice mail message. But you heard the trendy girls talking about his plans to get her to say nasty things about her best friend while the friend and the girls are listening in on a conference call.

- Leave it alone. You and your partner are not close enough for you to get on a powerful clique's bad side for her.
- Tell your partner the rumours you have heard. Ask her if, cute as he is, this boy is worth giving the mean girls leverage on her.
- Tell your partner's best friend not to trust the trendy girls and explain their plan.
- Confront the guy and ask why he is playing along with the clique to hurt your partner.

Continues . . .

6 **Clique Conflict**

Two of the cliques at your school don't like each other. They harass each other in the halls, paint graffiti on lockers, and post awful pictures and stories on their blogs. The principal and teachers are aware of the vandalism, but don't know which particular groups are involved.

- Stay out of it, and don't align yourself with either group.
- Leave an anonymous note for the principal.
- Go to the guidance counsellor to make it clear that the trouble involves two cliques, not individual people.
- Talk to the people you know in each group to see if there's any way of ending the conflict.

7 HANGIN' WITH A GANG

Your friend tells you that he is tired of being bullied and beat up at school by a clique. He is considering joining a gang in his neighbourhood to get some protection.

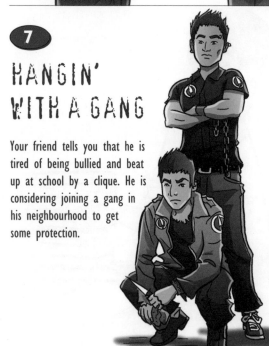

- Ask if you can do anything to lessen the pressure he is under at school.
- Tell him you will be with him as much as possible to avoid the clique.
- Talk to him seriously about what joining the gang would involve.
- Share some information with him from page 25 of this book.
- Help him think of alternatives to joining the gang, and ways to say "no" to them.

8 clique vs. couple

Your brother and his girlfriend belong to two conflicting cliques at school. Your brother's friends have asked you to cause trouble between him and his girlfriend so that everything can go back to normal.

- Do what your brother's friends suggest to keep your brother in good with his clique.
- Talk to your brother—tell him what his clique has asked, and ask him if he really cares enough about the girl to alienate his friends.
- Ask around and find out if the girlfriend's clique is against the couple, too. If it's important to both of them to stay in good with their friends, they might agree to cool it off without you having to torpedo their relationship.
- Support your brother and his girlfriend—love is more important than any clique.

9 SUICIDE CYBER-CLIQUE

There has been a lot of talk about a recent teen suicide at your school. You overhear a group of people in the lunchroom discussing websites that describe ways to kill yourself, and saying how cool it would be to join an online suicide club.

- Leave them alone; they're probably not serious about it.
- Tell the guidance counsellor what you've heard, and ask if the school can set up counselling for students who may need it.
- Watch for other students who are showing signs of depression or giving up.
- Tell your principal. The school authorities might want to look into cyber-cliques and their impact on students in your school.

10 TRUE BLUE TATTOO

Your friend has just been accepted into the rocker-girl clique at school. They say that she has to get a tattoo of the clique's name and "logo" on her arm to show her loyalty to the group.

- Help your friend research tattoos—the good and the bad. Look into the dangers of infection and what effect a tattoo will have on her image, now and in the future.
- Find out if she will get into big trouble with her parents. Remind her that since she isn't old enough to get a tattoo without a parent's permission, she will have to lie to get it.
- Remind her that a tattoo will be with her for life, unless she wants to go through an expensive and painful removal process. Tell her that once she has moved on to a different school, and eventually adulthood, she might not want to keep wearing her association with her old clique.
- Suggest she start out with a temporary tattoo in an obvious place to see if she likes the kind of attention it gets her.

31

More Help

It takes time and practice to learn the skills in this book. There are many ways to deal with cliques and with conflicts that arise because of them, but only you know what feels right for you in different situations. In the end, the best response is the one that pays off for everyone.

If you need more information or someone to talk to, these resources might help:

Helplines
Kids Help Phone (Canada)   1-800-668-6868
Youth Crisis Hotline (USA)   1-800-448-4663

Web sites
Canadian Safe School Network: www.cssn.org
Kids Help Phone: www.kidshelpphone.ca
How Cliques Make Kids Feel Left Out: kidshealth.org/kid/feeling/friend/clique.html
The Bully Lab: www.bullylab.com

Books
10 Things You Need to Know About Cliques by Jen Jones. Capstone Press, 2008.
A Is for Angst by Barbara Haworth-Attard. HarperCollins, 2007.
A Smart Girl's Guide to Friendship Troubles: Dealing With Fights, Being Left Out, and the Whole Popularity Thing by Patti Criswell. American Girl Publishing, 2003.
Cliques, Phonies, & Other Baloney by Trevor Romain. Free Spirit Publishing, 1998.
Egghead by Caroline Pignat. Red Deer Press, 2007.
Ghost Ride by Marina Cohen. Dundurn, 2009.
Impossible Things by Robin Stevenson. Orca, 2008.
Kindness by Dennis Foon. Playwrights Canada Press, 2010.
Little Black Lies by Tish Cohen. HarperCollins, 2009.
Me and the Blondes by Teresa Toten. Puffin Canada, 2006.
Mean Chicks, Cliques, and Dirty Tricks: A Real Girl's Guide to Getting Through It All, 2nd Ed. by Erika V. Shearin Karres. Adams Media, 2010.
Queen Bee by Chynna Clugston. Scholastic Inc., 2005.
Perfect Revenge by K.L. Denman. Orca, 2009.
The Present Tense of Prinny Murphy by Jill MacLean. Fitzhenry & Whiteside, 2009.
Rex Zero: The Great Pretender by Tim Wynne-Jones. Groundwood/House of Anansi, 2009.
Tribes by Arthur Slade. HarperCollins, 2002.

Video
It's a Girl's World. National Film Board, 2004
The Clique, 2008 (PG)
Mean Girls, 2004 (PG-13)
The Sleepover, 2004 (PG)
10 Things I Hate About You, 1999 (PG-13)

Some other titles in the Deal With It series
Cyberbullying: Deal with it and Ctrl Alt Delete it by Robyn MacEachern, illustrated by Geraldine Charette
Image: Deal with it from the inside out by Kat Mototsune, illustrated by Ben Shannon
Bullying: Deal with it before push comes to shove by Elaine Slavens, illustrated by Brooke Kerrigan
Girlness: Deal with it body and soul by Diane Peters, illustrated by Steven Murray
Peer Pressure: Deal with it without losing your cool by Elaine Slavens, illustrated by Ben Shannon

Special thanks to Wendy Craig, Ph.D., Professor, Department of Psychology, Queen's University for her review of this book.

Text copyright © 2010 by Kat Mototsune
Illustrations copyright © 2010 James Lorimer & Company
First Published in the United States in 2011

James Lorimer & Company Ltd., Publishers acknowledges the support of the Ontario Arts Council. We acknowledge the financial support of the Government of Canada through the Canada Book Fund for our publishing activities. We acknowledge the support of the Canada Council for the Arts for our publishing program. We acknowledge the Government of Ontario through the Ontario Media Development Corporation's Ontario Book Initiative.

Canada Council   Conseil des Arts
for the Arts   du Canada

ONTARIO ARTS COUNCIL
CONSEIL DES ARTS DE L'ONTARIO

Series design: Blair Kerrigan/Glyphics

Library and Archives Canada Cataloguing in Publication

Mototsune, Kat
    Cliques : deal with it using what you have inside / by Kat Mototsune; illustrated by Ben Shannon.

(Deal with it)
Issued also in an electronic format.
ISBN 978-1-55277-545-5 (bound).—
ISBN 978-1-55277-544-8 (pbk.)

    1. Cliques (Sociology)—Juvenile literature. 2. Interpersonal relations—Juvenile literature. I. Shannon, Ben II. Title. III. Series: Deal with it (Toronto, Ont.)

BF724.3.I58M68 2010   j158.2'5   C2010-905688-4

James Lorimer & Company Ltd., Publishers
317 Adelaide Street West, Suite #1002
Toronto, ON, Canada
M5V 1P9
www.lorimer.ca

Distributed in the United States by:
Orca Book Publishers
P.O. Box 468, Custer, WA
USA 98240-0468

Printed and bound in Hong Kong

Manufactured by Paramount Printing Company Limited in Tseung Kwan O, New Territories, Hong Kong.
Job number: 130767